What Is Left to Say

Cheryl Dumesnil

GLASS LYRE PRESS

Copyright © 2023 Cheryl Dumesnil
Paperback ISBN: 978-1-941783-95-5

All rights reserved: Except for the purpose of quoting brief passages for review, no part of this book may be reproduced or transmitted in any form or by any means, electronic or mechanical, including photocopying, recording, or by any information storage and retrieval system, without permission in writing from the publisher.

Design & Layout:	Steven Asmussen
Cover Art:	Cheryl Dumesnil
Author Photo:	Sarah Richmond

Glass Lyre Press, LLC
P.O. Box 2693
Glenview, IL 60025
www.GlassLyrePress.com

What Is Left to Say

for Sarah

and the Love that holds us

We sing. Our instruments are invisible. We carry them everywhere.

—Maeve O'Sullivan

Contents

I. Americana

Through	1
Americana	2
1. Cross Stitch	2
2. Folk Song	3
3. Quilt	4
4. Drum Corps	5
5. Barn Dance	6
"But who do you want as your neighbors?"	7
Use your voice	8
Fire Season	10
Today's Hymn	18
Spanish Lessons	19
Six Feet Apart	21
Betta splendens	22
Litany	25
Bible Study	26
It Keeps Happening	27
Forgive Me	28
This spring	29
What You Must Believe	31

II. Brood

Return	35
Today's Sermon	37
Brood	39
Instructions for Breaking	47

Home	49
Redwood Song	50
In Place	53
How to Carry a Flame	55
It Ain't Pretty	58
A Dissertation on Quantum Entanglement as a Love Song	59
Open	61
Scatter	62

III. Dissolve

Dissolve	65
1. Prologue	65
2. Twig	66
3. Smoke	70
4. Drought	74
5. Feather	77
6. Sky	80
7. Atom	83
8. Shell	86
9. Wing	87
10. Breeze	91

Notes	95
Acknowledgements	97
About the Author	101

I. Americana

*you might as well answer the door, my child
the truth is furiously knocking.*

—Lucille Clifton

Through

The river is frozen. We are skating
down the center. Horrible things

are happening on the banks.
On both sides. *Grab my hand.*

Terror is a vapor rising off rocks,
off trees. I'm not looking. I'm

blurring my peripheral vision.
Keep going. I'm focused on the spot

ahead, where perspective narrows
the river until the banks kiss.

The vanishing point. *Come on
now, grab my hand. Grab*

anyone's hand. I don't know
where we'll be when we get there.

Americana

1. Cross Stitch

The crow's call retreats
        into its throat, and trees

rescind their chlorophyll,
        and the red-blue-red lights

withdraw their stains
        from the curtains,

and nothing remains
        but that ghost of a leaf—

a bit of brown lace
        slicked to a shiny black boot.

2. Folk Song

What is left to say
when lies

have removed
our tongues?

Not a hint of
sweetness in the milk

seeping from
the cut fig's stem.

3. Quilt

Today's pattern
will stitch together

glasswing butterflies,
razor wire crowns,

and apologies for
its sentimentality.

The children are sleeping
under foil blankets

on concrete slabs,
urine-damp and unable

to touch each other.
What calculus

solves for X • Y =
a six-year-old

defending herself
in immigration court

when she should be
making foil crowns

and dreaming
of glass wings

lifting her skyward?

4. Drum Corps

The cardinal dives
into her own reflection

defending her territory,
mistaking *Self* for

Enemy. Again and
again, whole-body

collisions pounding
the sheet glass

like a bass drum
while the growing

crowd shouts:
Someone stop her—

someone stop her or
she'll break her neck.

5. Barn Dance

Today's caller takes the shape
    of a child who emerged

from the fault line
    after the earthquake

everyone knew would
    come. Her cobweb

teeth, her leaded eyes—
    she carries a lambskin

scroll we all need to read
    but we're busy tallying

our damages, waiting
    for the underwriter

while the hold music drones,
    while the hold music drones.

"But who do you want as your neighbors?"

The one who made her scarf into a baby sling
and carried her toddler three hundred miles on foot.

The one who salvaged four planks from a lean-to,
turned a bedsheet into a sail, and called it a boat.

The one who filled the babies' bellies with songs
about the food they could eat when they got there.

The ones who crossed the ocean in a '51 Chevy pickup
fastened to oil drum pontoons. The ones who

lashed plastic bottles to a grid of bamboo stalks
and christened it *Hope*. The one who poured his last

drops of water between his sister's chapped lips.
The ones who whispered: *keep going, almost there,*

a few more days. The one who taped the soles
of her broken shoes onto a stranger's bleeding feet.

The one who made room on the crowded train roof
for more ones. The ones who travelled together

because we're safer that way. The ones who
made mattresses of their bodies so their children

could sleep, who ignored the rocks gouging into
their backs by counting innumerable stars.

Use your voice

      the stones said,
their amber glow
      the only light
in the infinite
      dark. They
unzipped her
      throat, removed
the clay bird,
      and placed it
between her
      teeth. *May you*
feel loved
      by something
greater than
      yourself. May you
find purpose
      to drive you
forward. May you
      burn pain as
fuel to grow

beyond your

worst fears,

    she sang

to anyone

    who would listen.

Fire Season

Fifty miles southwest of the fire line
we smell the burn and expect refugees
to arrive any moment—jays swooping
down from the mountain, bewildered
deer sniffing the air. What can we offer
but a handful of acorns and empathy?
Why would they trust us anyway?

*

On Highway 49, a billboard spells out
Yosemite Valley Closed in lights orange
as the sun behind this scrim of smoke.

*

They name the fires
Ferguson, Mendocino Complex, Carr,
and we watch the statistics rise:
57,846 acres; 74,408 acres; 100,154 acres
0%, 3%, 9% contained.

*

From evacuees, words like *hellfire, end times*.

*

Cause: vehicle mechanical failure
could mean a tractor backfired, or

an old carburetor emitted a spark,
which means it could just as easily

have been me who pulled my ailing
Mercury Lynx off the road and left it

idling too long over the tinder box.
Except when my mechanic removed

the converter cover, she warned me
not to drive into a field of dry weeds.

Which means the difference between
a blue sky and an octogenarian

huddled under a wet blanket
with her two great-grandbabies,

all of them dead, could be
the right words at the right time,

a bit of dumb luck.

*

Their mama said,

*I'm sure my grandma
did the best she could
to take care of my babies.*

I'm sure she did.

*

In crews named after their tools—
First Saw, Second Saw, Pulaski, McLeod—
inmate firefighters set the line,

clearing fuel between the flames
and that 4000-square-foot home,
or that stand of old-growth trees,

earning $2.43 an hour and maybe
an American flag presented
to a loved one at the funeral.

*

Cars inch down the mountain
on melting tires.

Embers rain on windshields.
A white truck's flank toasts brown.

Through a wall of flames
is no longer a metaphor.

*

Today's Camp Fire update:
84 fatalities, 560 missing, 70% contained.

I'm afraid it's going to get worse.
It's going to get much, much worse.

*

A man recovers his deceased
      mother's engagement ring
           from an ash heap and calls

the charred jewelry box
      a miracle—the impeccable
           diamond, a swirl of rose gold.

*

Cause: a hammer strikes a nail head.

Cause: a cigarette flies out a car window.

Cause: a lawnmower scythes a rock.

Cause: a windblown powerline falls
on the 236th day without rain.

*

The school bus driver
ripped his shirt

into pieces he doused
with water

for the children
to hold over their mouths

as the door's
rubber seal burned.

It's my first week on the job,
he said. What else

are you gonna do?
I kept driving.

*

The black cow grazing the blackened hillside
would be invisible if not for her flank

rippling as she steps forward, nosing the ash.
What can she expect to find? The only

bovine for miles in this charcoal on charcoal
sketch set against a parchment sky.

*

Air quality experts recommend
N95 facemasks to filter out

microscopic bits of family
snapshots, noxious chemicals,

green card documentation,
a kindergartener's handprint,

her grandfather's mandolin.

*

Today's good news
is the toddler

wearing a red dress
and fire fighter rainboots,

handing burritos
to the line crew

while her mother films
and the Internet sighs.

*

What's left
when fire

reduces
all you own

to ash
the flood

lifts and
sluices

downstream?

*

Smoke presses this truth against the sky:
either your home is on fire, or you're pulling
someone else's tragedy into your lungs.

*

We force our chests to rise.

*

I'm not going to tell you
Manzanita seed dormancy

is partially broken by fire.
I'm not going to tell you

Manzanita seedlings
appear in large numbers

during the postfire spring.
Scientists predict

there is no postfire—just
blue skies 'til next time, just

ink, transcribing the ache.

Today's Hymn

is slop buckets knocking against each other
and a towel cart squeaking down the hall

and grease stains worked into cracked
palms   is red-wing blackbirds dive-bombing

a raven with yolk on its beak   is dragging
grace around like a rust-eaten wagon

pretending it's whole   is spring leaves
as tiny soldiers receiving soot with open hands

is a fifteen-dollar garage sale bike and now
the kid can ride to school like everyone else

Spanish Lessons

The flyer tacked up
in the break room

reads *Know Your Rights*
in English and Spanish.

How do you say
Do you have a warrant

signed by a judge?
How do you say

Tell them nothing?
How do you say

I will call for help?
Alfonso's tomato plants,

grown from seeds
his abuela sent,

flourish in the soil
between our homes.

How do you say
I will water them

while you're away?
How do you say

*When you slice
one open, the whole*

of us bleeds?

Six Feet Apart

Height of a grandchild   depth
      of a grave   enough water

to drown in   twice the length
      of my reach   an eagle's

wingspan   a canyon
      with no echo   a measure

of longing we cannot
      cross   the distance

between blossom and
      blackberry staining your teeth.

Betta splendens

Crop the image right,
and the neon blue scales

become stepstones
disappearing

into a red and black
tailfin reminiscent

of a theater curtain,
as in *pay no attention*

to the man behind the . . .
Or, rotated ninety

degrees, the fin becomes
a bull fighter's cape

in mid-twirl, crimson dare
to a beast manipulated

to charge. It is a lie
that two male Bettas

placed on opposite sides
of Lake Erie would

find each other
and fight to the death,

though it is true
that no domestic tank

is big enough
to accommodate them

thanks to natural
territorialism and selective

breeding for aggression
begun by 18th century

children who scooped
their predecessors

out of rice paddies
and watched them spar

in a bucket until a winner
prevailed. This is why

Betta splendens—beautiful
warrior—is now found

in single-occupancy cells
stacked on pet store shelves—

bright gems, sad divos
hanging motionless

in pint containers labeled
rosetail, dragon scale,

veil tail, half-moon,
and half-sun. *They have*

evolved to withstand
difficult conditions—

minimal water, low oxygen,
the acne-pocked employee

explains, then assures
the worried customer:

No, they don't get lonely,
and *Yes, it's for their*

own good. They would
kill each other if they could.

Litany

Stitch a tally mark
for each breaking—

black thread
through burlap.

Are we counting
or mending?

A needle vibrates
between

fingertips; a train
telegraphs

its arrival, miles
down the track.

Bible Study

Truly I tell you,

                The life expectancy

whatever you do

                for transgender women of color

for these sisters of mine,

                living in the United States

that you do unto me.

                is thirty-one years old.

Matthew 25:40

It Keeps Happening

Mid-June, snow
      is choking
           the crocus patch.

Her ribcage
      is wrought iron,
           immoveable

against her breath.
      Her words were
           the soft knock

of tumblers
      falling into place
           as the safecracker

turned the dial.
      It happens
           all the time now—

those purple
      mouths frozen
           open and dying.

Forgive Me

Is it possible
that Love,

which is
too small
an answer,

is also the
only answer?

This spring

Equinox 2020

is my wife's sweating
        nightmares and that man

waiting at the bus stop
        with a gas mask strapped

to his face and the green
        hillside which is fire

season in the making,
        and my neighbor who

reports another break-in
        in broad daylight, and *Is*

this the new normal?
        the radio asks, and this

spring is empty drug store
        shelves where rubbing

alcohol and flu remedies
        used to be, and this

spring is *four gallons of*
        bottled water for every

family member and *do not*
        panic and *this is not*

a drill, and this spring is
        furlough and *layoff*

and *non-essential* and
        voters who don't think

a woman is electable—
        and these are female

voters, the radio says—
        and this spring is *Next up:*

a Bay Area chef
        who lives in a minivan

with two kids because
        she can't afford rent,

and this spring
        is a near-dead fig tree

turning new leaves
        to the sun, which is

in no way an answer, but
        still, I stop driving and

look up for a while.

What You Must Believe

As a mound of dust and a mouthful of spit
is to a brick,

as that one spit-and-dust brick
is to a wall

is to a shelter for a family
fed by one pot

hung over a fire tended all day
and all night, too—

this, my love,
is how you will survive—

as a spoon scraping concrete
is to escape—

no matter how they try
to break you.

II. Brood

"The land knows you, even when you are lost."

—**Robin** Wall Kimmerer

Return

The doctor has removed
        my femur and carried it

to a table across the room.
        I am awake, but not in pain.

The doctor is a white coat
        turned away from me.

I hear a sound not unlike
        the buzz of a tattoo gun.

Above me hang the usual
        flood lights encased in steel.

In their curved reflections,
        my leg is a coin purse

snapped open, a gaping mouth
        crayoned red. *That time will*

never come again is a song
        the radio sings as the doctor

returns, holding my bone
        like a majorette's baton,

rotating it to reveal an image
        she's carved: the teenager

I once was, sitting beside
        Emily Dickinson's grave.

There's the boiled wool coat
        I wore all year, my scuffed

black boots. *Forever is*
        composed of nows is the song

the doctor hums as she
        snaps my bone in place.

There's the acorn I left
        on her tombstone.

Here's the prayer
        I whispered to the leaves.

Today's Sermon

Lake Tahoe, 2019

is Cock and Bull beer caps
under the picnic table

and the mountain jay
cussing out the ground squirrel

and the ancient lake
holding boulders like secrets

is cigarette butts
wedged between pavers

leading to the Port-O-Let
above Emerald Bay

is the woman crouched
behind the tour van

while sobbing loudly
in the universal language for

I'm afraid of something
I do not understand

is a speedboat circling the island
like a scalpel excising a tumor

is the child's bare arms
in a thirty-degree breeze

and her father cupping his
hand around the match

is the rock that told my palm
when you learn to love

what is ugly, only then
will you find peace

is last year's charred pines
standing sentry on the mountain

and a master colorist painting
more blues than I can name.

Brood

> *"Scientists discovered over 1,000 females, many brooding eggs, in a shimmering 'octopus garden.'"*
> **—National Geographic**

Out there—two miles
below the surface:

octopuses, *hundreds*
nestled in a rocky outcrop,

at the base of an underwater
mountain. In footage

from a remote-controlled
submersible, they take

the shape of Fabergé
eggs—their bodies inverted,

undersides exposed,
arms draped like filigree

down the contours of
their pewter heads.

*

"Octopus's Garden"
is a Beatles song

written by Ringo Starr

under his birth name,

Richard Starkey.
George Harrison,

seen in a documentary
helping Starr

work the song out
on the piano,

later insisted,
It's Ringo's song.

*It's the second song
he's ever written,*

mind you, and it's lovely.

*

Cephalopod, likely
Muusoctopus robustus.

*This inside-out pose
is common among*

*females protecting
their growing young.*

*

To Brood, verb:
    (of a fish, frog, or invertebrate)
    to hold developing eggs in the body

    (of a bird) to sit on eggs to hatch them

    (of a human) to think deeply about
    something that makes one unhappy

*

*The idea for the song came to Starr
on Peter Sellers' boat in 1968.
He had asked for fish and chips
for lunch but got squid instead.*
It was okay, *he said.* A bit rubbery.
Tasted like chicken. *The captain
told Starr octopuses travel along
the sea floor, picking up stones and
shiny objects for their gardens.
Starr would later admit the song
was further inspired by his desire
to escape mounting hostility
among The Beatles.* I just wanted
to be under the sea, too, *he said.*

*

Brooding, adjective

darkly somber
> a *brooding* landscape

> a quiet, *brooding* atmosphere

> *brooding*, violent images reminiscent of film noir

*

According to scientist Chad King,
The water appeared to shimmer

in places where the octopuses
concentrated, like an oasis

or a heatwave off the pavement.
Warmth, says King, *may be seeping*

out of the seamount, creating
optimum conditions for incubation.

It definitely looked like
the octopuses wanted to be there.

*

Brooding, adjective:

moodily or sullenly thoughtful or serious

    a *brooding* genius
    a *brooding*, embittered man

*

The song gets very deep into the listener's consciousness,
Harrison explained, *because it's so peaceful. Ringo
is writing cosmic songs these days without even realizing it.*

*

Do not mistake
the exposed pink

star of my center
for vulnerability.

Try it, you will
regret it, their arms,

cocked and ready,
appear to say.

*

The discovery came just months after
scientists reported the only other
nursery on record: *I would have sworn*
our observations were a once-in-a-lifetime

opportunity, says biologist Janet Voight.
Makes me think there are a lot more
places like this than I ever dared imagine.

*

Brood, noun:

a family of animals produced at one hatching

    a *brood* of chicks

    her *brood* of pups

    synonyms: offspring, progeny, young

*

The submersible's camera
spotted *tiny embryos*

cradled in their mothers' arms.
If you look closely, you can

just make out the eye
of a developing embryo,

which means these eggs
are doing well, says Voight,

or at least that one is.

*

The song, which contains the lyrics
Oh what joy for every girl and boy

Knowing they're happy and they're safe,
is sometimes thought of as a children's ditty.

Fact: The track required thirty-two
takes before the band was satisfied.

Fact: It was the last song The Beatles
released with Ringo on lead vocals.

Fact: It has been performed by the Muppets
in several episodes of their shows.

*

They turn themselves inside out
to protect their young,

I tell my wife over dinner
as our kids play catch

in the backyard. She nods
in recognition. October smoke

paints the sunset every shade

of orange, purple, pink.

*

Thousands of expectant mothers
congregated, brooding.

*

Not everyone agrees the shimmering
indicates heat, though Voight confirmed

the first garden *did, indeed, have warm
fluid billowing up from the seafloor.*

Bruce Robison counters, *It's unlikely
there's any heat involved.* He posits

a seepage of methane gas. Says Voight:
This observation is further proof we have

no idea what's going on in the deep sea.

Instructions for Breaking

Listen   there has always been light
there has always been a congregation of lights

there has always been a place in the dark
where we'll meet you

there has always been a handprint
pressed into a wall   over the prints

of those who arrived before   under
the hands of those who will follow

waiting for yours   there has always been
will always be   a voice calling

against the cacophony of voices   your name
until you hear it and sing it back to us

Listen   there have always been
wing beats and heartbeats   and spoons

whipping batter in bowls   and fists
kneading dough   and truth as the wind

has chosen to tell it   and the tapping
of one finger on a desk in the lamplight

while everyone else sleeps   Love
you must   listen for the coordinates

place and time   when the next gathering
begins is always now   join us or do not

but hear me   you are never alone

Home

Sunlight glides along silk threads
strung between the weeds.

A snapped branch caught by its tree
is a bass clef framing the lake.

Once I came here to tell the water
all I couldn't say. I watched

three swallows fly east; only
two returned. They answered

none of my questions. But this
morning, the forest breathes

openly, silver webs lifting and falling
as our sheets do while you sleep,

and I hear them before I see them:
two spooked deer bounding

toward the clearing, escaping
something apparently more dangerous

than me, because they stopped right
here, belly-high in the chicory,

and lowered their mouths to graze.

Redwood Song

When you wake and the knot in your belly
is the redwood burl that tripped you

on yesterday's trail, then you breathe
and the knot unfurls the worry that your

mother has stopped singing. *Has she
stopped singing?* Your mother who took her first

voice lesson at age seventy-three and
skipped across the parking lot afterward

because it felt that good to raise the voice
you have loved since before you were

born. *Is she singing?* Look outside: how
sunlight paints those redwoods grown

so close to one another they could have
split from the same trunk, though

the slender one clearly is younger than her
darker twin. See how their branches

entangle each other's bodies in a slow
dance, this pair, how the one whispers in her

other's ear: *Are you singing?* Close your eyes—
feel her bark brushing soft as your mother's

hair against your cheek, feel the weight
of her head on your shoulder where it won't

always be, feel your arms forming that
circle of trees that will stand with the absence

of their mother in the center, and suddenly
you hear it: *Everything you ever needed to know*

you learned from giant sequoias, which
sounds as stupid as it does true—how all

the tallest have been tested by fire, how
the whole forest stands because their shallow

roots have intertwined underground,
how when you step inside the tree's hollow,

place your hand on her charred ribcage,
she will tell you, *Thank you.* She will say,

Stop worrying. She will say, *Everyone
is going to be okay (if you are willing*

to adjust your definition of okay),
then she will say, *It is you who needs*

to keep singing, and the mountain jay
with its roughed up blue crest will

51

pick up the chorus: *Keep singing. Are you singing? You need to keep singing.*

In Place

On the sixth day, I soak
cotton balls in peppermint oil

and push them into dirt mounds
the gophers have disrupted

in the garden, their tunnels drawn
from one blueberry bush

to the next, like the unsteady
lines of a kindergartener's

dot-to-dot. *How will we feed
the hungry children now*

that the schools have closed?
In the house, my wife attends

an online tutorial about
food-borne pathogens

while across the yard our kids
sift through gravel beneath

the trampoline, picking out
magnetic words scattered

by last night's wind:
kindle   grace   fierce ly

The gophers—I don't know
if they're after worms

or the roots of these bushes
teeming with white blossoms

and baby blues. I sprinkle oil
at the base of each plant

just in case, then join the kids
searching through pebbles:

utopia   in   your   apocalyptic

mouth

How to Carry a Flame

Sepia, jaundice, no—
bathwater after

the last dusty child
has been lifted

and wrapped.
A meteorologist

drags her pen
across the stratum:

smoke layer, fog,
smoke, cloud layer,

more smoke—
and it gets harder

to imagine
robin's egg,

Wedgewood,
iris, sea glass,

the nose of a plane
pushing out

above the gloom.
My eyes—who

insist they know
something about

time—ache
with the effort

to draw in
noon's light.

*If depression
were a color . . .*

Cornea, macula,
retina, lens.

*How much longer
can this last?*

Even the headlines
are trafficking

in rhyme: *foreboding,
orange, smoke-*

choked skies.
I study the candle

flickering on my desk—
black wick anchoring

its tiny sun,
like a thumbtack

skewers memory
to a map. I will

my body to become
its glow, to carry

that shimmer
in my cells—*for as*

long as it takes—
as I did you, Love,

all those years
you were gone.

It Ain't Pretty

Before the miracle
of symmetry and wings,

that caterpillar
spent days gorging

and shitting, spinning
webs she would climb

to the pinnacle
underside of a leaf,

where she hung herself
upside-down then

peeled off her skin
and liquified inside

a straightjacket
of her own making.

That's right—
before she released

into full-bore flutter
and grace, what she

left behind was
a massacre scene.

A Dissertation on Quantum Entanglement as a Love Song

I whispered your name in a napkin,
crumpled it into my palm and opened

an empty hand. I poured our story
in a coffee mug and buried it

in the weeds behind the park bench.
A love so secret I refused to tell it

even to myself. I dreamed we kissed
in the cafeteria line while the steward

looked away. I sang you loudly
in my empty car, mountain storm

slicking the roads. *Stay home,*
the ocean, who never lies, told me,

so I did. Runner, I imagined my words
becoming the beat in your ears.

I dreamed your shoes beneath my bed.
Your wet paint tenderness.

Your shimmer like water held
at the brink of over-spilling the cup.

The sun, who is always right, aimed
her compass point at my chest

and said, *Wait, you'll be amazed.*
Years gone, your scent woven

through the cables of a thrift shop
cardigan. *I wished you well under*

the changing colors of a sourwood tree—
your words arrived not like a dam

burst, more like a rhythm I had
never noticed pulsing in my throat.

Open

How the honeybee
flies ever more frantically

against the screen
this morning. How the one

star casts its light
93 million miles to touch

your face. This is what
I'm talking about:

the love that tries all your life
to find you. Open

the sash. Sunlight
and shadow shivering across

your unmade bed.

Scatter

How many have told me
      when they turned the urn

upside down, the wind
      refused the ash, blowing

their beloveds back home?
      Enough for me to promise,

Love, when it happens,
      I will not close my eyes,

but open my mouth
      to lift what's left of you

off the breeze with my tongue.

III. Dissolve

*Inside this new love, die.
Your way begins on the other side.*

—Rumi

Dissolve

I. Prologue

*Sparrow song dredges her body
from the water dream. Swamp-dark*

*gives way to light. She lies on the bank,
naked, cuneiform of leaches*

*nursing at her skin. One by one,
the birds wing down, tug*

*the bloodsuckers, and fly off,
onyx curls pinched in their beaks.*

*

Dear Sparrow,

For years the voice in my dreams:

*Something extraordinary
is about to happen.
Just wait. You'll see.*

Dear Sparrow,

each morning I wake
sore from the waiting.

2. Twig

Dear Sparrow,

The scrub jay keeps stealing my blueberries.

Only the ripe ones.

It's a drought year, and the crop is so small.

I've tried tying silver ribbons to the branches, like they do in the vineyards, but it's not working.

Every day, a few more gone.

I ate some bitter pink, just so I could say I tasted them.

*

Tell the scrub jay:
Eat them if you must.

May they color your wings
a deeper blue.

*

Dear Sparrow,

In the dream, I gave birth
        to a baby girl small as
                the palm of my hand,

translucent skin stretched
        over tiny bones. Her hip blades,
                the nodes of her spine—

they reminded me
        of the day my mother
                sliced a cooked chicken

open: dark architecture
        of vertebrae and ribs,
                the day I stopped

eating meat. Sparrow,
        this baby's bones tasted
                like starvation. Sparrow,

the baby's name was Delight.

*

Remember:

*As a child you imagined
gravity releasing you*

*gently from its grip,
your body falling*

*slowly through space,
past planets and stars.*

*When you sensed
an imminent landing,*

*No, you would whisper,
only falling.*

*

Dear Sparrow,

The scrub jay has returned with companions.
Flock of blue, sky in motion, threading the trees.

Never have I seen so many in one place.

One by one they are taking my berries—
a beak opens, a beak closes, a tug, a release.

*

You've always hated scrub jays? Why would you say that?

The caw that rips open morning.

The silver chest bared to the sunrise.

The raiding of nests, the shattering of eggs.

Like tympany, that flair of blue wings.

*

*How do you feel about releasing
that twig you are grasping,*

*finger by finger, until there's
nothing left in your hands?*

*How do you feel
              about falling?*

3. Smoke

Dear Sparrow,

The forest is on fire again.
The homes are filled

with smoke. The mothers
of the dead are still

aching. Dear Sparrow,
wind has tattered

the roadside tents
and still there's no place

to go. Dear Sparrow,
I don't know how

to stay awake inside
all this breaking.

*

*The space between
your breaths—*

*that is where
you will find yourself.*

*

Make something new,
the canyon echoes.

Make everything
                       new.

*

Is anything really new? she asks, fitting the grappling hook
into a crevice, giving the rope a yank.

                See it: rock painted by time—
                sand, charcoal, rust,
                sand, charcoal, rust.

Hasn't earth recycled the same drops of water for millennia?
she asks, lowering her body, hand under hand, toward the river below.

*See the river
excavating
the canyon floor.*

*Amniotic fluid, ocean, stream—what's the difference?
A molecule of Neanderthal tear
shows up in a water glass in Poughkeepsie, New York.*

*The chaos of atoms
vibrating it all—
can you see it?*

The seeing is new.

*

Was it *The Sparrow & the Egg*
or *The Sparrow & the Twig*—
the name of that song in the dream?

*

You choose:

>   *Sparrow: spirit, bird, arrow.*
>
>   *Twig: what's gripped before flying.*
>
>   *Egg: what's held in the body, and then—*

4. Drought

Dear Sparrow,

1:08 a.m., I woke
to the sound of rain.

First a few drops
on the skylight, then a polite

applause of leaves,
then water sluicing

through the gutters,
the downspout gargling.

Sparrow, summer rain
never happens here.

A three-year drought
ending. I fell back to sleep

smiling. Sparrow,
when I opened my eyes

the ground was dry.

*

*Look around: the gardenia,
the society garlic, the bleeding*

*heart, even the hydrangea
in her meager wisps*

*of shade—three years
of drought and they've all*

*found a way to keep
blooming, the act of blooming*

encoded in their DNA.
                        And you?

*

Sparrow is
       pecking at the sheet

(which is your skin)
       draped over the bars of her cage.

(which are your ribs)
       When I wake I feel her

(stuck and fluttering)
        under my left breast.

*

*How many times are you willing
to let go? Until the last rung slips*

*from your hand? Until the only thing left
is you who have been here all along?*

5. Feather

Dear Sparrow,

The child has cancer.
The child is dying
of cancer. This can't happen.

But it does—

*of starvation, of car crash
of bullets, of rage . . .*

*It can happen. It is
happening. It has
happened. It has always
happened. It will
continue happening . . .*

*

Now what?

Sparrow:

When
the

worst
thing
has
happened,
and
you
are
still
standing—

what then?

*

Dear Sparrow,

Too large for her body, the hearse waits at the curb.
Barn swallows stitch in and out under chapel eaves.

The child-body sinks into the earth.
The birds sing: okay, okay, okay.

The birds dive in and out of their mud nests.
The birds lift their faces to the sky.

The child rests in her grave.
The birds continue to sing: okay, okay, okay.

*

Remember:

*You are a feather
released, a canoe
designed
to ride the breeze.*

6. Sky

In the dream, weeding the garden—
the tug and snap of roots,

the clover and the clover and the clover.
Turned earth smells of blood.

The notable absence of worms.
In the dream, the women haunt

the manzanita shade—
their collective, thrumming ache—

and you tell them—how dare
you tell them—*Loss is not*

the problem. The story—this
can't happen—is the problem.

The problem is believing
you are the one who holds up the sky.

*

In the dream she said,
If you leap, the safety net will appear.

So I launched off the cliff,
and Sparrow,

I haven't stopped falling.

*

She kept her promise. Don't you see?

*

Dear Sparrow,

In the dream, the ring
the child had given me

broke—metal snapped
at its thinnest point,

fire opals disintegrating
in their settings.

I told the child, *What matters
most is not the ring,*

*but that which remains
after the ring is gone.*

*Dear Sparrow, I'm afraid
I won't see her again.*

*

*Breathe into the absence.
The absence
will make you whole.*

7. Atom

Atom, atomos—

indivisible; that which
cannot be cut.

We thought.

For how long
did we believe

we were whole?

*

*The problem is believing in anything
but the chemical substrate*

of light + bird song + rain.

*The equation of a moment
becoming itself.*

*

Light + Bird Song + Rain =

we are ever-changing
collections of atoms

orbited by incomplete
numbers longing for more.

*

The seeing. The seeing is new.

*

Dear Sparrow,

Last night, I picked the final blueberries and placed them along the fence top.

You would like to know how many? I can't recall how many.

Only how the silver ribbons glimmered in moonlight, the nearly imperceptible breeze.

Only how the berries glowed like planets waiting for birds.

*

*Let me tell you—the way
you will be living*

from this day forward

*will have nothing to do
with the way you have*

lived until now.

                    Are you ready?

8. Shell

The red-winged blackbird, red-winged blackbird
the phoebe the phoebe the phoebe
the raven the raven the raven—all day long.

I walked down to the creek, waded in and pulled
at cattails, loosing clogs to release the flooding.

A tufted titmouse picked bugs off a branch.
A hummer shadow seared across my path.
The dove's full-throated moan.

> *Do you want to be the Sparrow or the Egg?*

Yes, Sparrow—I heard you calling.
Yes, Egg—I left your shell on the compost heap.
Forgive me, I am somewhere in between.

9. Wing

Have I told you
    the story of your birth?

The midwife said, We have to
    get the baby out—now.

Your mother inhaled
    the dark. Your mother bore

down. Your mother dove
    down, tunneled down,

soared down to the center
    of the earth. Your mother

gathered the infinite
    elders who have birthed

and birthed and birthed.
    Like kindling, she bundled

their strength, then pointed
    up and launched, surged,

jetted, shot upward
    toward the crust, toward—

Take her! Take her!
    the midwife crowed.

Your mother's hands
    pulled you from the wake.

Mother arms. Mother ribs.
    Mother heart. Mother

breast. You were born
    with one arm punched

forward, fist clenched—
    a superhero, flying. Flying.

You were born flying.

*

Have I told you about the cherry tree?

How the mother worried and worried for her sickly infant who nursed all night but withered by day.

How she rocked in the dark hours, her shrinking bird-baby swaddled in her arms.

How her eyelids fluttered shut for a moment, and the cherry tree appeared: pink-white, luminescent.

How peace grew alive in her, from the roots of her feet to the trunk of her torso to the branches of her arms to the blossoms of her hair.

How from that day forward, she knew she was God?

Everything she touched: rocking chair, swaddling blanket, child, dark—God?

*

*Remember when the priest said God is light
and wherever there is light, there is God,*

and you stared at the red sphere hanging above the altar, confused, the candle flickering inside?

*

*Remember when the priest said
God is love, and you smelled your mother's perfume*

*wafting down from the choir loft
as she opened her chest in song,*

and it almost made sense?

*

*Remember when the priest said God
is the breeze, and you saw her fingers*

*combing through the cherry orchard,
white petals lifting off in flocks,*

and then you believed?

10. Breeze

Black-tailed deer, malachite,
southwesterly breeze.

The upswell of breath
expanding the robin's chest,

feathers refracting copper
in the morning light.

Only this, my love, is real.

The single atom buzzing
in the constellation of buzzing

that makes up a twig
or a sparrow or an egg.

This moment becoming itself.

*

Dear Sparrow,

I want nothing more than cherry petals
falling on my upturned face.

*

*The night-blooming jasmine,
its crepe-white star—*

this, my love, will have to do.

Notes

"Fire Season" includes direct quotations from live interviews with survivors of the Camp Fire in Paradise, California.

"Bible Study" is a found poem sourced from The Holy Bible and a commonly quoted statistic.

"Return" was inspired by Gloria Anzaldúa's *Borderlands/LaFrontera*, particularly these words I read as a twenty-year-old, which have never left me: "When I write, it feels like I'm carving bone. It feels like I'm creating my own face, my own heart—a Nahuatl concept. My soul makes itself through the creative act." The line "Forever—is composed of Nows—" is the first line of Emily Dickinson's poem 690 and "That it will never come again" is the first line of poem 1741.

"Brood" includes language found in Jason Bittel's article, "World's largest deep-sea octopus nursery discovered" on nationalgeographic.com and wikipedia.com's entry on the song "Octopus's Garden."

"Instructions for Breaking" was written on the occasion of Brett Kavanaugh's appointment to the United States Supreme Court.

"How to Carry a Flame" includes an excerpt from a headline that appeared in the *San Francisco Chronicle* on September 9, 2020: "Bay area transfixed by foreboding, orange, smoke-choked skies."

"A Dissertation on Quantum Entanglement as a Love Song" is for Sarah.

Acknowledgements

Thank you to the editors of the following journals for publishing these poems (or earlier versions of them):

The American Journal of Poetry, "Brood"

Baltimore Review, "A Dissertation on Quantum Entanglement as a Love Song"

Gravitas, "It Ain't Pretty" and "Use your voice"

Headline Poetry, "In Place"

Metamorphosis, "Drum Corps" (as "Again") and "Quilt" (as "Today's Poem")

NiftyLit, "Barn Dance" and "But who do you want as your neighbors?"

Ninth Letter, excerpts of "Dissolve" (as "The Sparrow and the Twig")

Not Very Quiet, "Today's Sermon" (as "Sermon I")

The Racket, "Through" and "Return" (as "Carve")

Rattle, "Today's Hymn" (as "Today's Sermon")

Redheaded Stepchild, "It Keeps Happening"

Rise Up Review, "Spanish Lessons"

Rogue Agent, excerpts of "Dissolve" (as "The Sparrow and the Twig")

Signal House Edition, "How to Carry a Flame"

Sisyphus, "Fire Season"

Sparkle + Blink, "Forgive Me"

What Rough Beast, "This spring"

Writers Resist, "Bible Study" and "What You Must Believe"

"Open" appears in the anthology *Without a Doubt: Poems Illuminating Faith*, edited by Raymond Hammond, published by New York Quarterly.

Epigraphs:

Maeve O'Sullivan's "Vocal Chords" appears in *Vocal Chords*, Alba Publishing, 2014.

Lucille Clifton's "the light that came to lucille clifton" appears in *good woman*, BOA Editions, Ltd., 1987.

Robin Wall Kimmerer's quotation appears in the essay "An Offering," collected in *Braiding Sweetgrass*, Milkweed Editions, 2013.

Rumi's "Quietness" appears in *The Essential Rumi*, translations by Coleman Barks with John Moyne, Harper Collins, 1995.

Author Photo Credit: Sarah Richmond

Special thanks to the following writers, for their encouragement as this book was taking shape: Sean Thomas Dougherty, Diane Dreher, Susan Goldberg, Domenica Ruta, Deema Shehabi, Aaron Smith, and Katie Mauro Zeigler; to Janice Deitner, Phil Dumesnil, Brennan Dumesnil-Vickers, and Kian Dumesnil-Vickers for design feedback; to LaDonna and Gabby, Joe and Hedda, Heather and Bruce, and Michele and Dom, for providing the quiet retreats where many of these poems came to life; and to Sarah Richmond for all of the above, as well as her inspiration, insight, tenderness, unending love, and fierce support.

About the Author

Cheryl Dumesnil is the author of the poetry collection *Showtime at the Ministry of Lost Causes;* the 2009 Agnes Lynch Starrett Poetry Prize winner, *In Praise of Falling;* and a memoir, *Love Song for Baby X.* A social worker and freelance writer, she lives in the San Francisco Bay Area with her wife Sarah and sons Brennan and Kian, where she practices living slow in a high-speed world.

exceptional works to replenish the spirit

Glass Lyre Press is an independent literary publisher interested in technically accomplished, stylistically distinct, and original work. Glass Lyre seeks diverse writers that possess a dynamic aesthetic and an ability to emotionally and intellectually engage a wide audience of readers.

Glass Lyre's vision is to connect the world through language and art. We hope to expand the scope of poetry and short fiction for the general reader through exceptionally well-written books, which evoke emotion, provide insight, and resonate with the human spirit.

Poetry Collections
Poetry Chapbooks
Select Short & Flash Fiction
Anthologies

www.GlassLyrePress.com

www.ingramcontent.com/pod-product-compliance
Lightning Source LLC
Chambersburg PA
CBHW022008120526
44592CB00034B/745